BAD, BAD GERMS-
STAY AWAY!!!

(by Nurse Lorraine)

Green Amoeba

Written by:
Lorraine Connolly RN

Copyright © 2022 Lorraine Connolly RN.
Illustrated by: Lorraine Connolly & Jackie Murphy

All rights reserved. No part of this book may be reproduced, stored, or transmitted by any means—whether auditory, graphic, mechanical, or electronic—without written permission of both publisher and author, except in the case of brief excerpts used in critical articles and reviews. Unauthorized reproduction of any part of this work is illegal and is punishable by law.

ISBN: 979-8-88640-361-9 (sc)
ISBN: 979-8-88640-362-6 (hc)
ISBN: 979-8-88640-363-3 (e)

Because of the dynamic nature of the Internet, any web addresses or links contained in this book may have changed since publication and may no longer be valid. The views expressed in this work are solely those of the author and do not necessarily reflect the views of the publisher, and the publisher hereby disclaims any responsibility for them.

One Galleria Blvd., Suite 1900, Metairie, LA 70001
1-888-421-2397

BAD, BAD GERMS- STAY AWAY!!!

(by Nurse Lorraine)

Written by:
Lorraine Connolly RN

About the Author

Lorraine Connolly is a Registered Nurse. She is also a mother. She has a message to deliver to children about germs but adults will also benefits from learning her message once again.

About the Illustrator

Jackie Murphy is a second year double major in Art and Communications at UNH. Both Jackie and Lorraine's families reside in the same New England neighborhood.

Some germs are good.

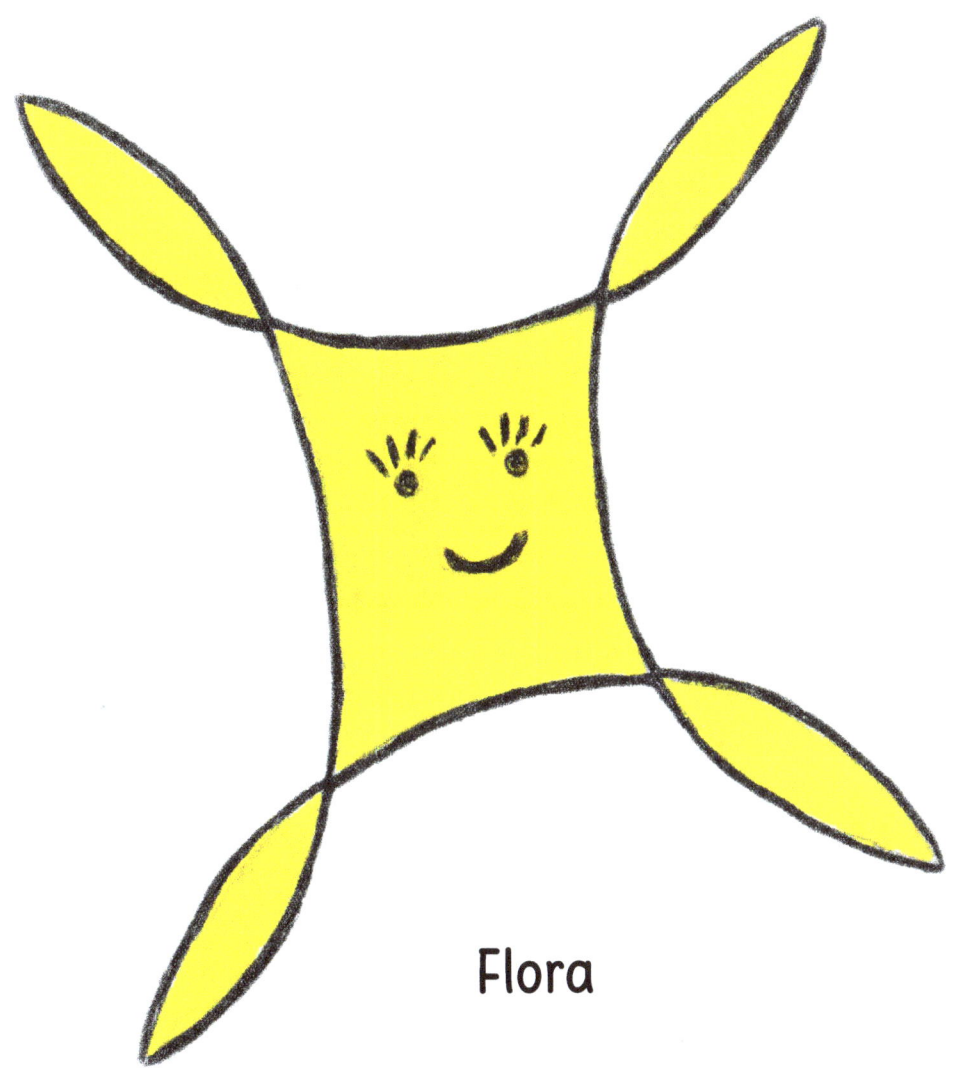

Flora

But some germs are bad.

The Green Amoeba

The bad germs make us sick!

But we're the boss of our bodies!

How do we keep the bad germs away?

Green Amoeba, STAY AWAY!
I keep my fingers off my face
I wash my hands, I wash my hands
And wash the bad germs down the drain!

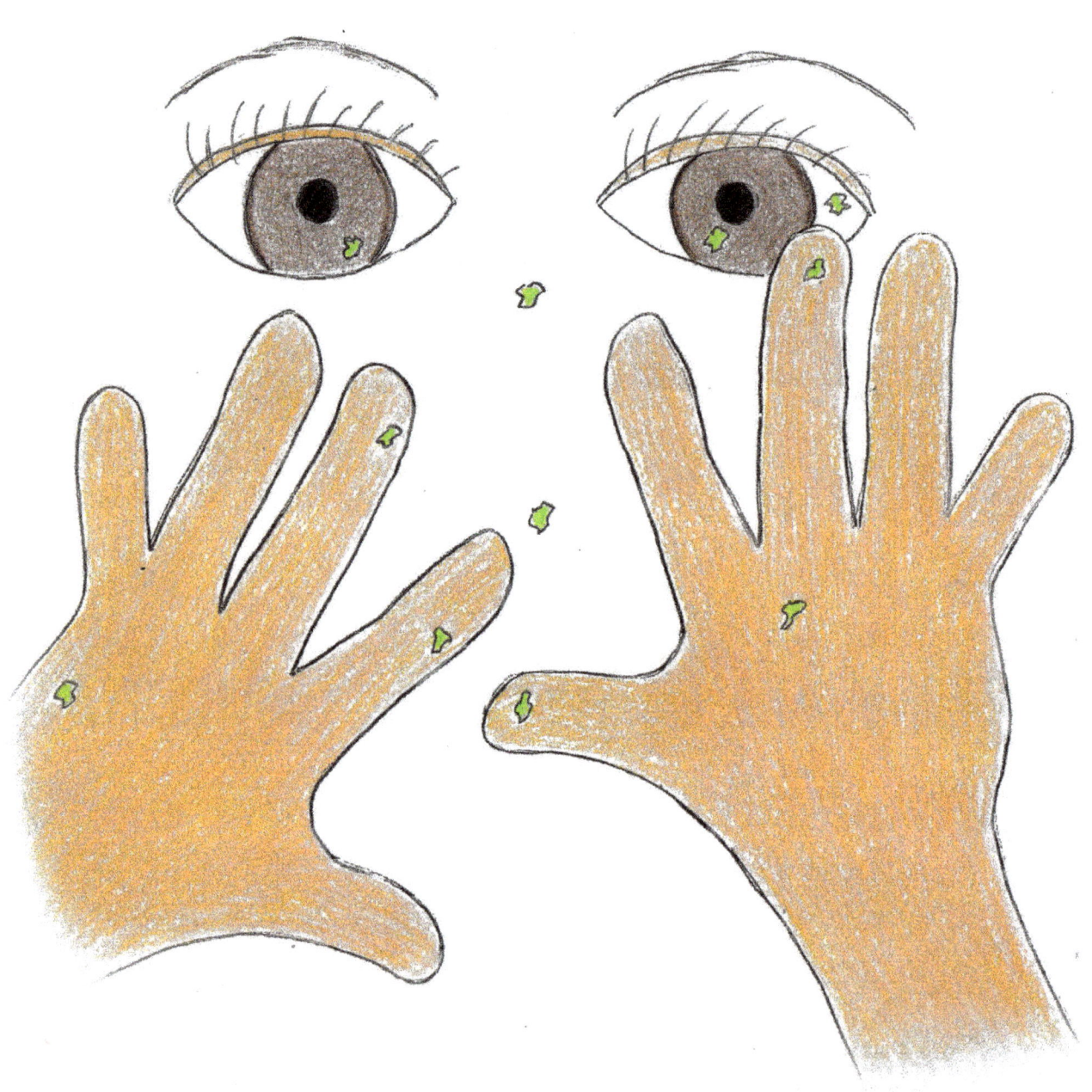

Green Amoeba, I won't let you get inside
I won't put my fingers near my eyes.

Green Amoeba, STAY AWAY!
I keep my fingers off my face
I wash my hands, I wash my hands
And wash the bad germs down the drain!

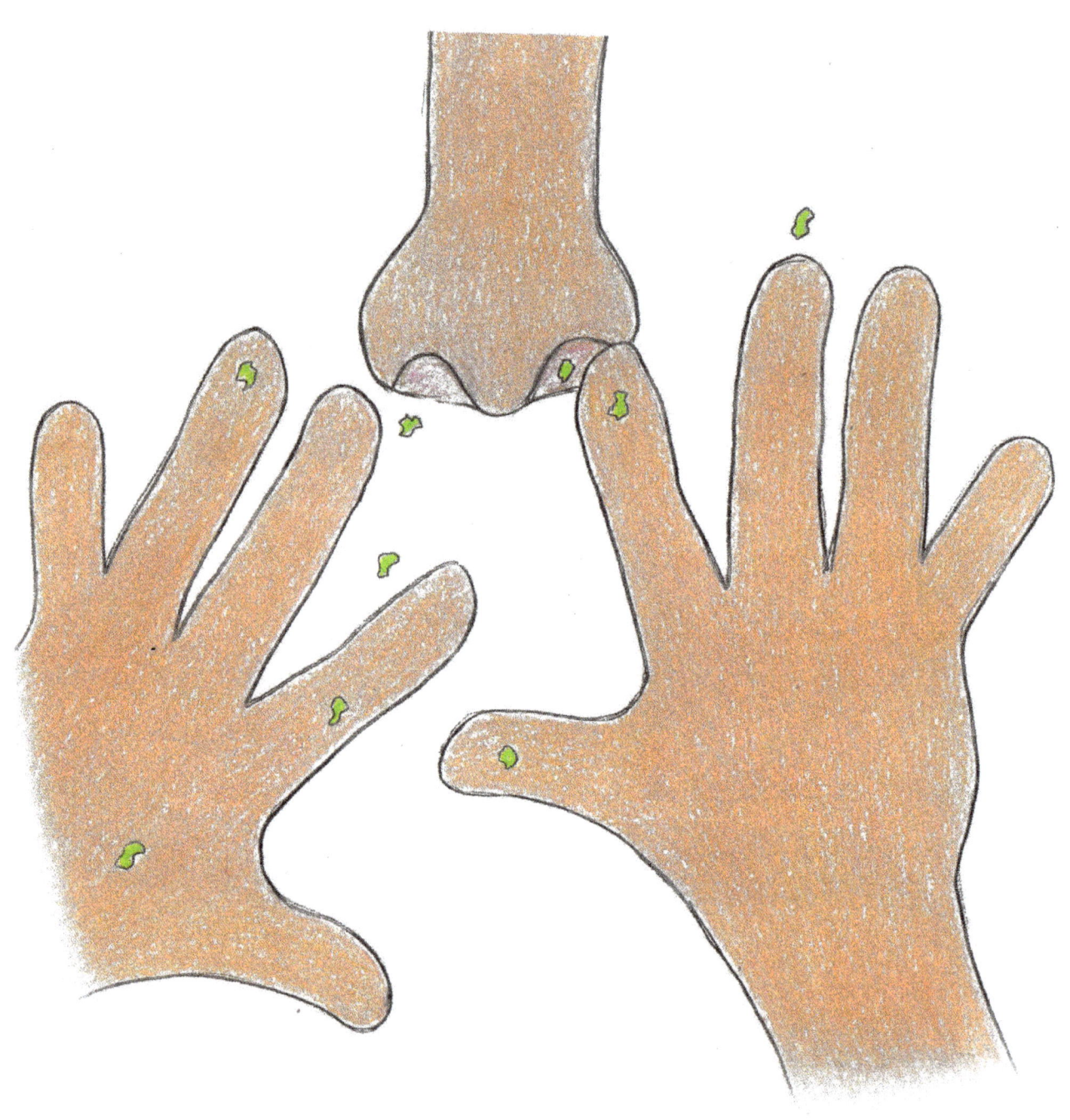

Green Amoeba, the door is closed
I won't put my fingers in my nose.

Green Amoeba, STAY AWAY!
I keep my fingers off my face
I wash my hands, I wash my hands
And wash the bad germs down the drain!

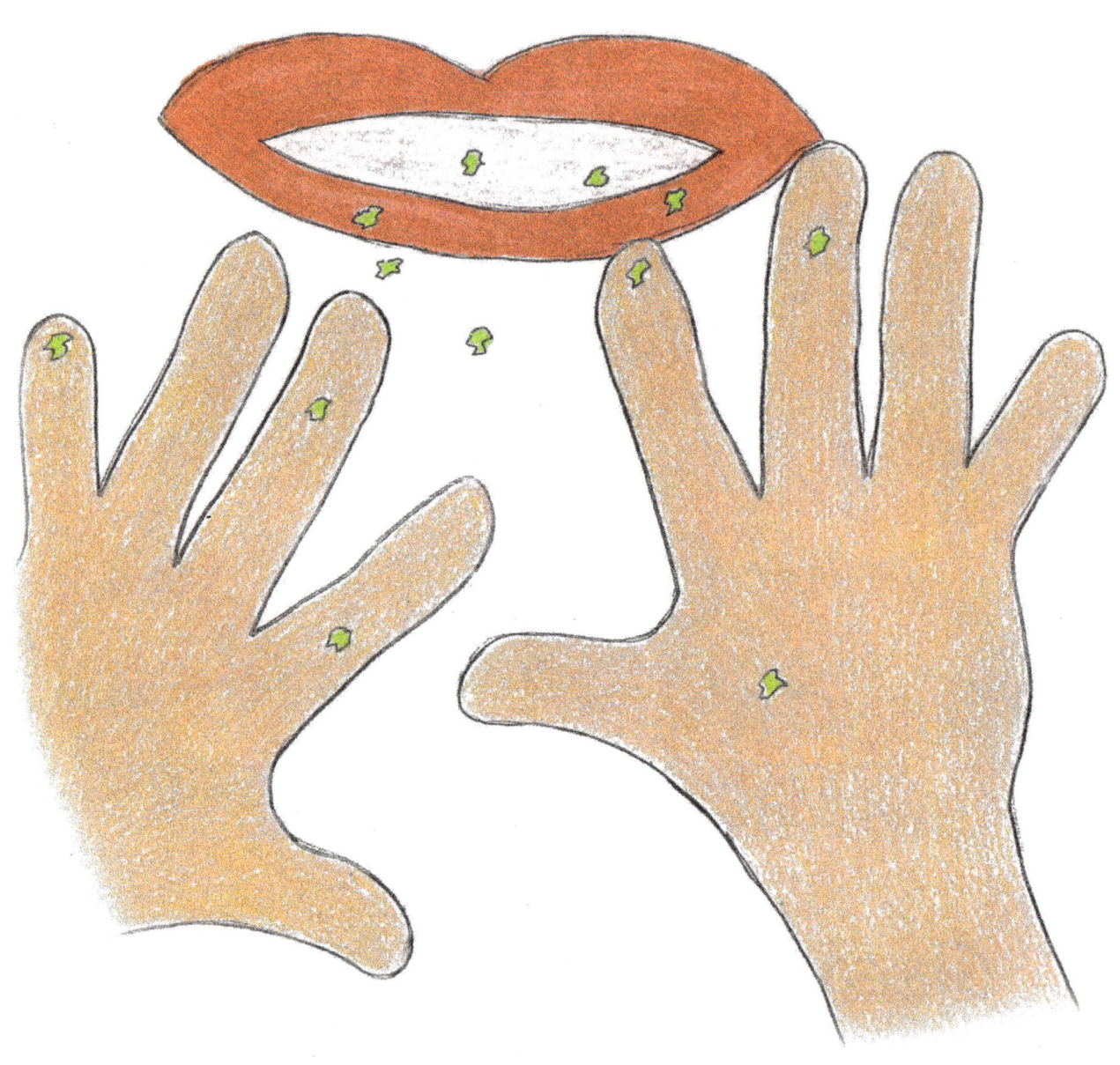

Green Amoeba, I'm going to keep you out
I won't put my fingers near my mouth.

Green Amoeba, STAY AWAY!
I keep my fingers off my face
I wash my hands, I wash my hands
And wash the bad germs down the drain!

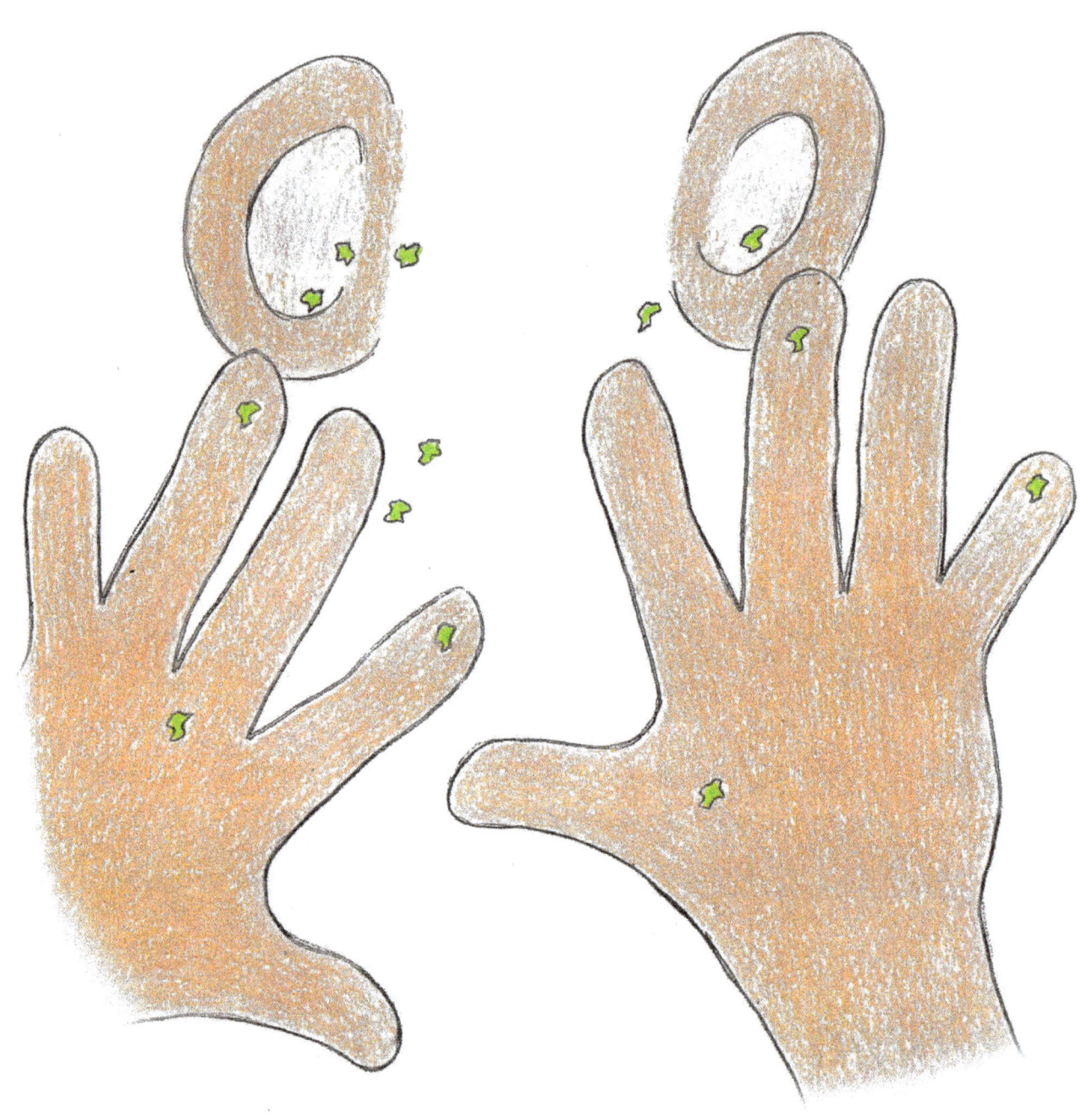

Green Amoeba, do you hear
I won't put my fingers in my ears

Green Amoeba, STAY AWAY!
I keep my fingers off my face
I wash my hands, I wash my hands
And wash the bad germs down the drain!

Green Amoeba, STAY AWAY from:

my eyes

my nose

my mouth

my ears

Bye Bye, Green Amoeba!

The End

www.ingramcontent.com/pod-product-compliance
Lightning Source LLC
LaVergne TN
LVHW072123060526
838201LV00068B/4962